Sam Fillmore

THE FIRST
SONATINA BOOK
FOR THE PIANO

EDITED BY WILLARD A. PALMER

INTRODUCTION TO THE SONATINA

The *sonatina* has been defined as a diminutive *sonata*. In many respects the *sonatina* may serve to acquaint the student with the basics of musical form and style that are characteristic of the classical *sonata*.

A *sonatina* usually has 2 or 3 rather short movements. While these movements provide contrasts of tempo and mood, they also complement one another, combining to fulfill the overall plan for a complete work in several parts.

A *sonatina* movement is generally constructed from two themes or subjects:
> 1. the principal theme (A)
> 2. the subordinate theme (B)

These themes are often used in the simple two-part (binary) form A B, which may, because of repeats, become A A B B or A B A B. Some movements are in three-part (ternary) form, A B A. By the use of repeats, this may become A A B A or A B A B A. A short ending phrase, called the *codetta*, is sometimes added to complete a movement in any of these forms.

The student should be taught to recognize and identify the principal and subordinate themes as well as transitional phrases between the two themes, and any short developments of thematic material that may occur. He should also be able to identify the *codetta*. Application of this type of analysis to the *sonatinas* contained in this book will also provide the student with a basic understanding of the elements of composition.

CONTENTS

Second Edition

Copyright © MCMXCIII by Alfred Publishing Co., Inc.
All rights reserved.   Printed in USA.

Cover art: A detail from An Architect's Table
by Pierre-Charles Duvivier (French, 1716–1788)
Oil on canvas, 40⅛" x 31", 1772
Norton Simon Art Foundation, Pasadena, California

Sonatina in C Major

T. Latour

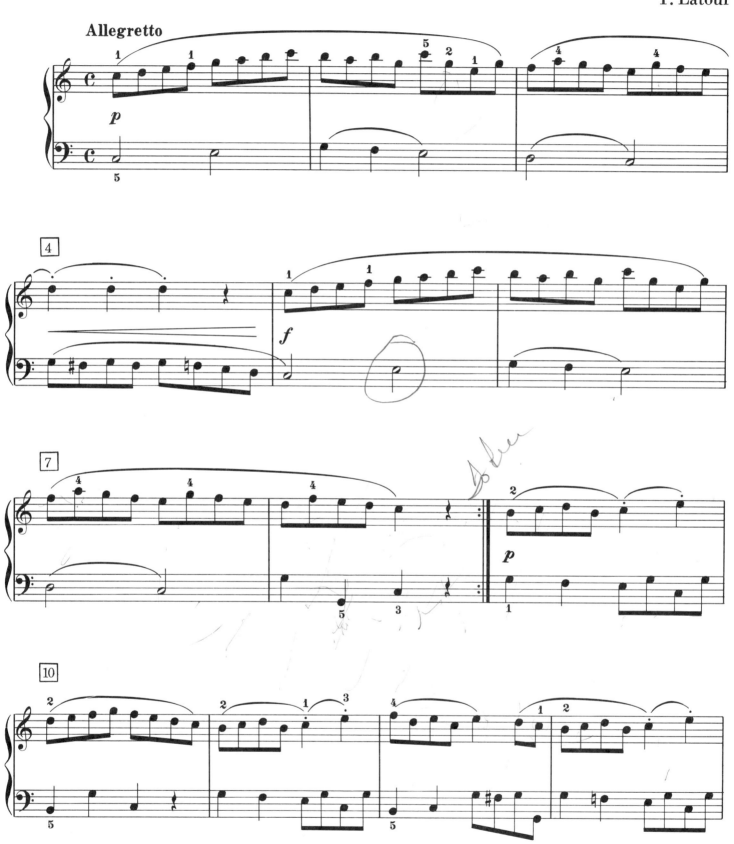

Latour was pianist and composer to King George IV of England during the early part of the 19th century.

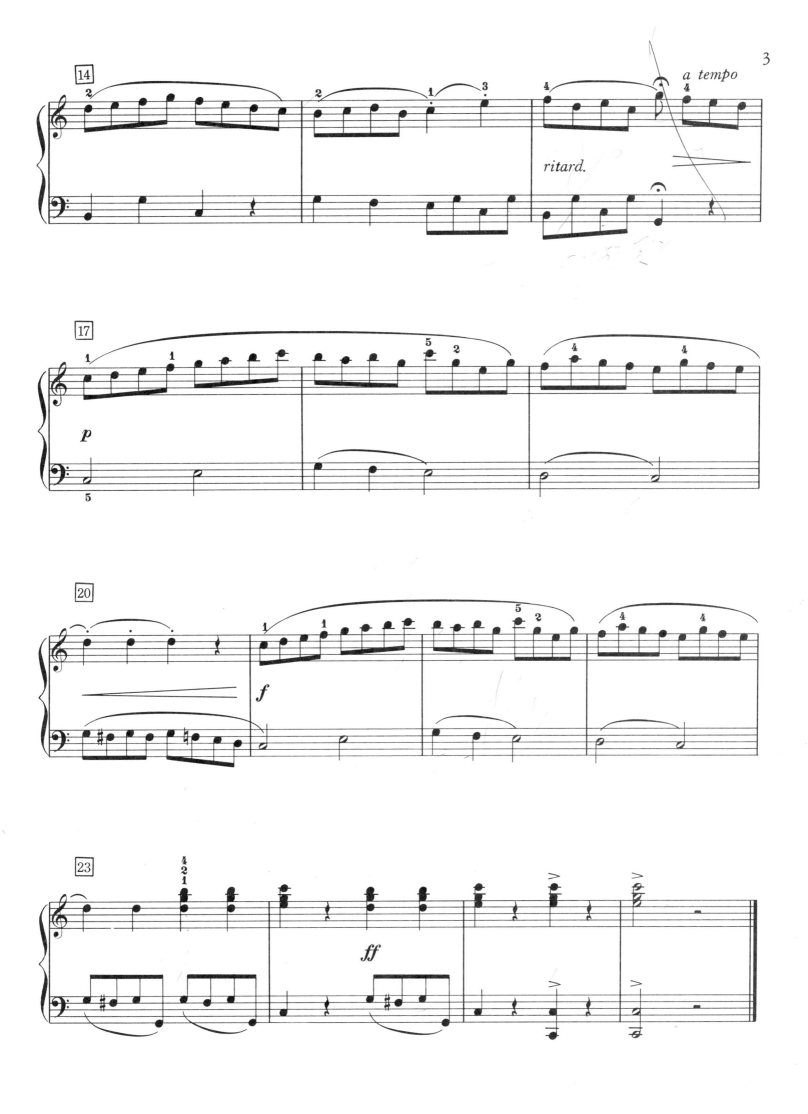

Pastorale
Andante

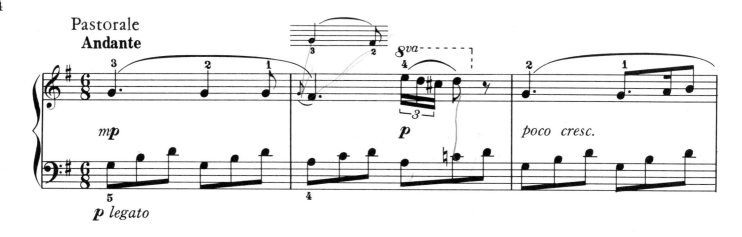

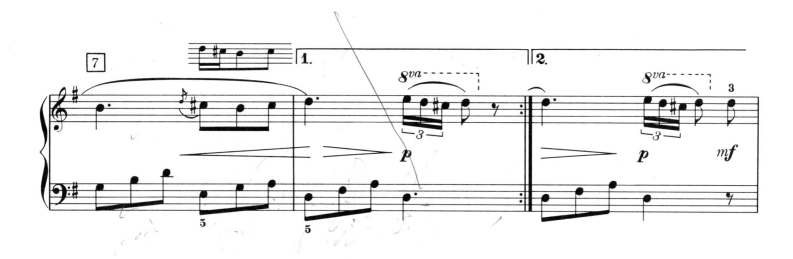

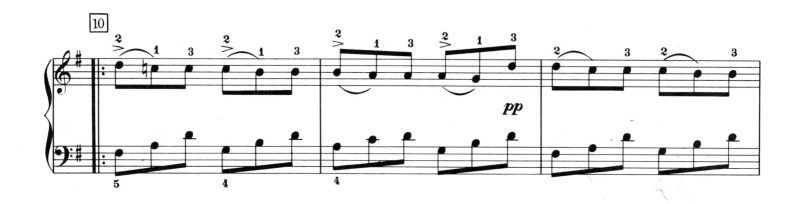

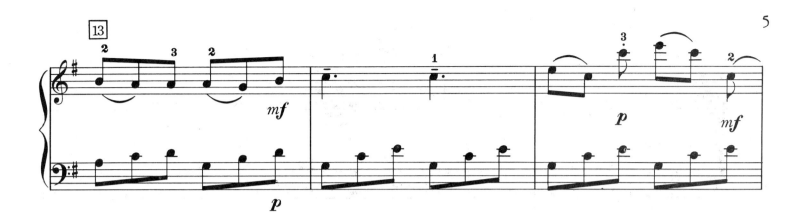

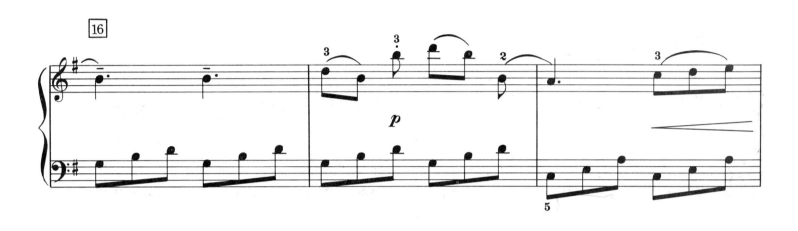

6

Rondo
Allegretto

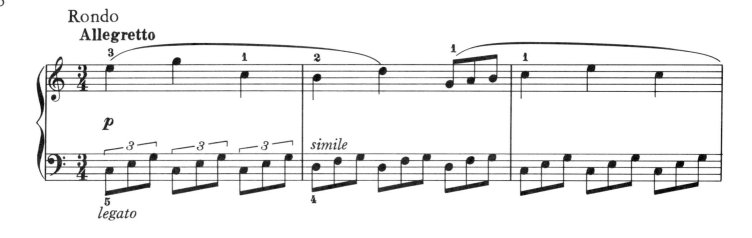

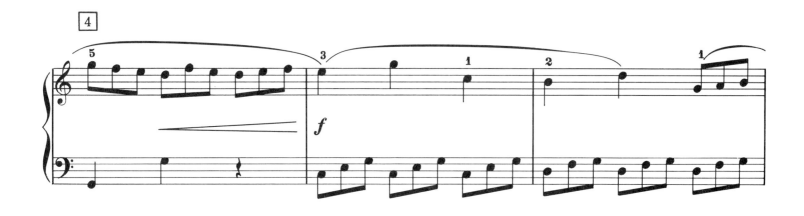

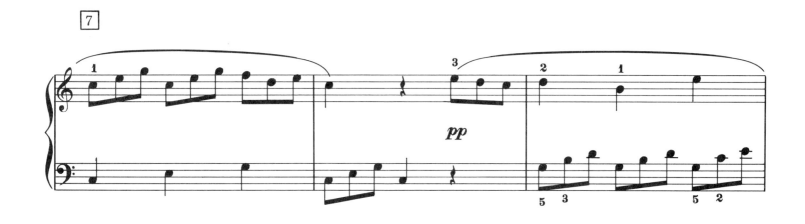

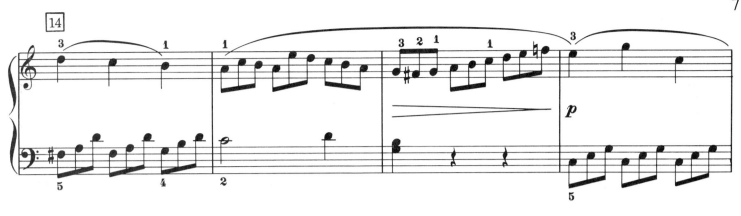

Sonatina in F

Johann Baptist Wanhal
(1739-1813)

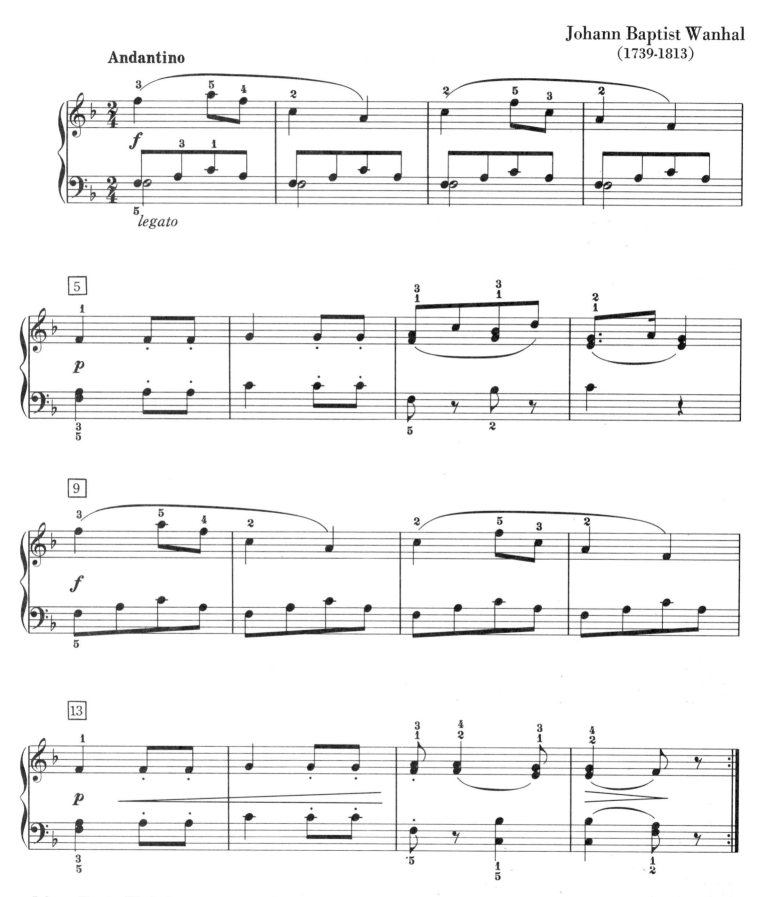

Johann Baptist Wanhal wrote over 70 volumes of piano music. He also wrote more than 100 symphonies and as many string quartets, plus numerous choral works. His music was very popular during his lifetime.

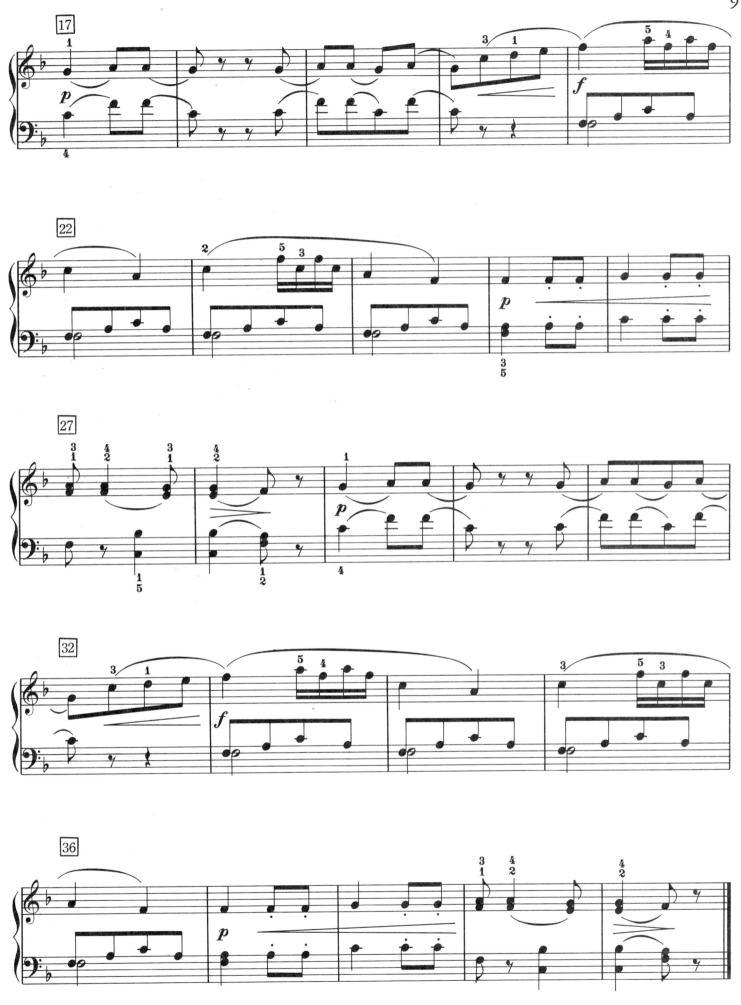

10

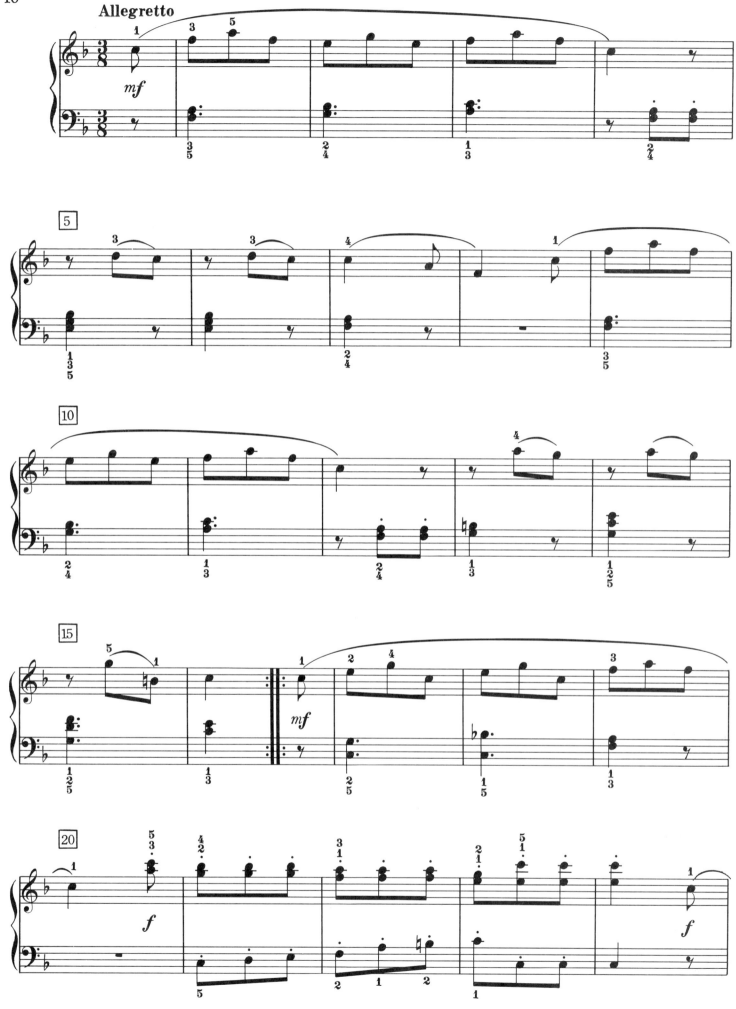

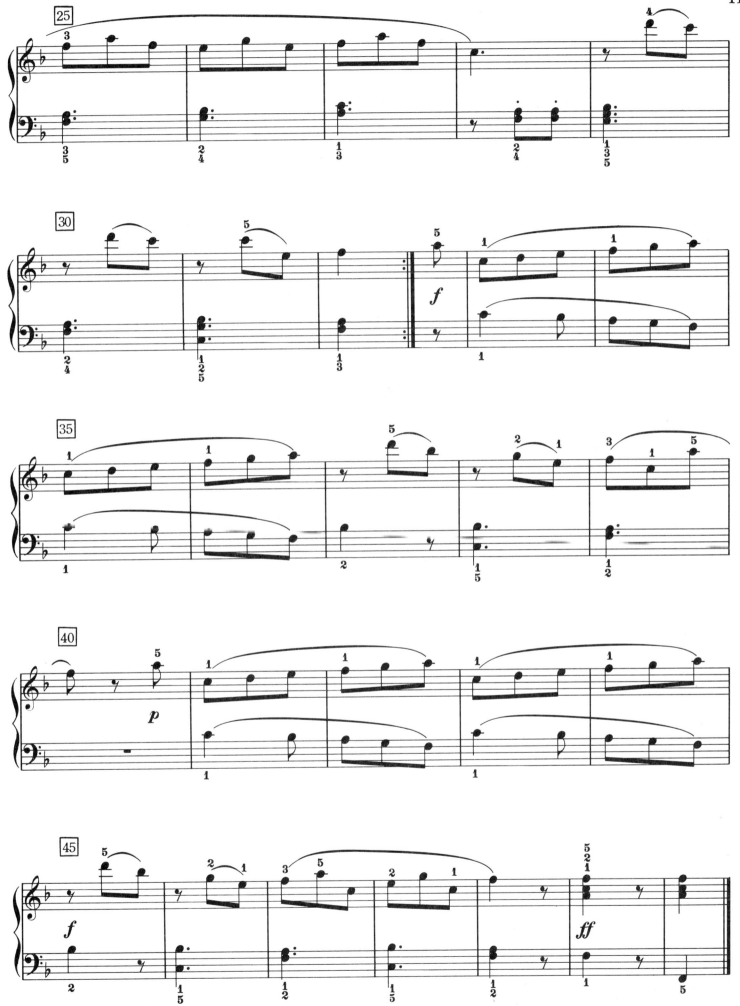

Sonatina in C Major

Tobias Haslinger
(1787-1842)

Tobias Haslinger was an Austrian music publisher. He was a very likable person and was a close friend of many composers, including Beethoven, who held him in high esteem.

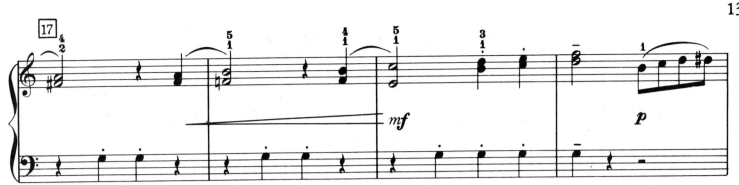

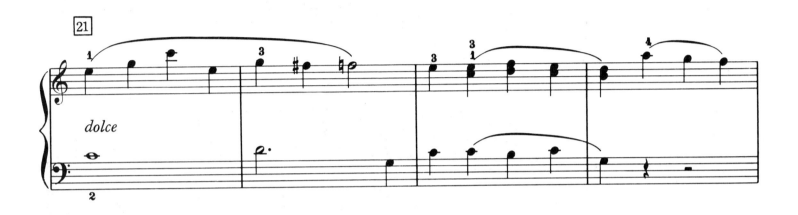

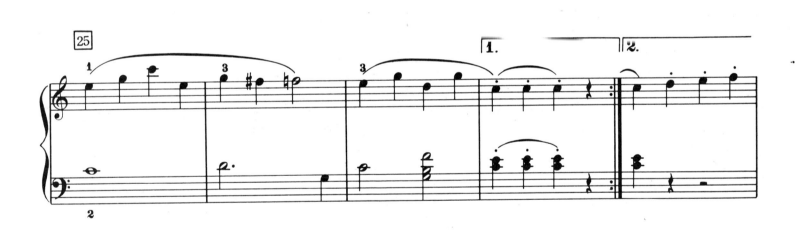

Allegretto

p giocoso

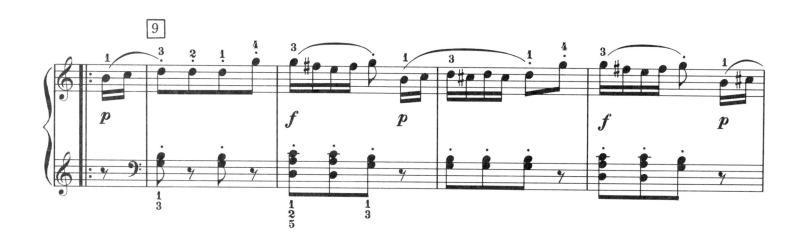

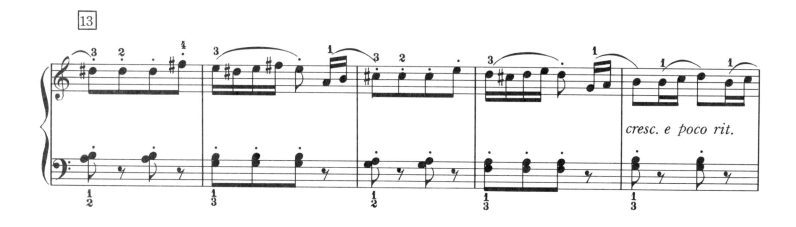

cresc. e poco rit.

15

Sonatina in G

Ludwig van Beethoven
(1770-1827)

Ludwig van Beethoven was one of the greatest composers of all time. He brought the symphonic form to its full maturity. As a pianist he was phenomenal. His 32 piano sonatas contain some of the most wonderful piano music ever composed.

Romanze

Sonatina in C Major

Muzio Clementi, Op. 36, No. 1
(1752-1832)

Muzio Clementi was one of the most famous musicians of his time. His playing rivaled that of Mozart. He was highly respected by Beethoven. Chopin used Clementi's famous method book, *THE ART OF PLAYING ON THE PIANO-FORTE*, with all of his beginning students.

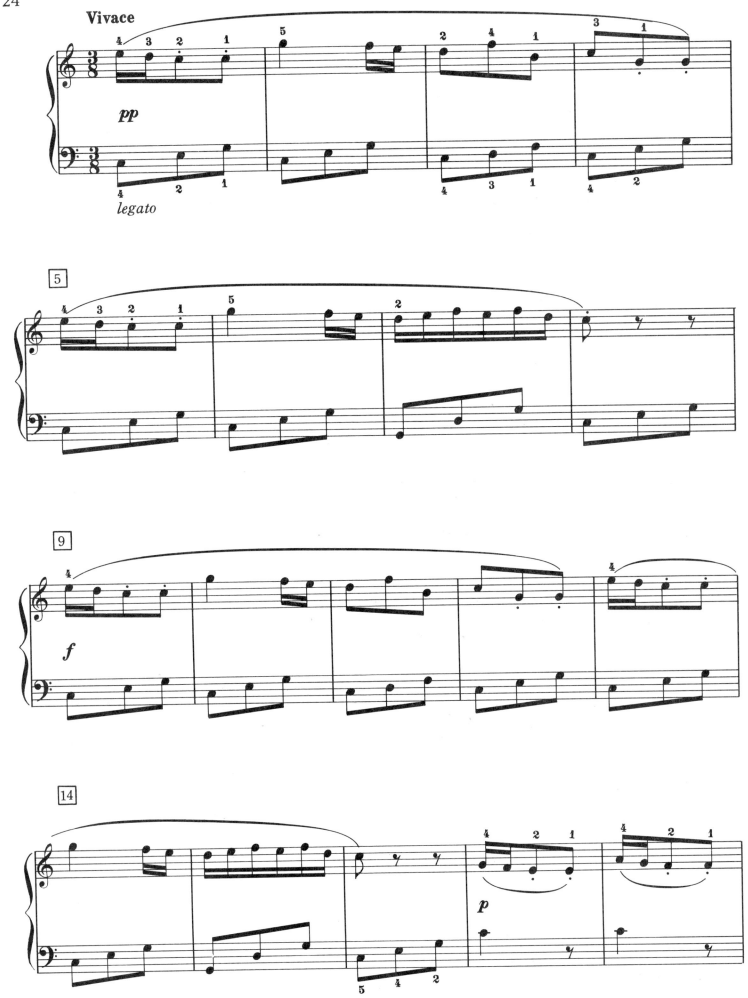

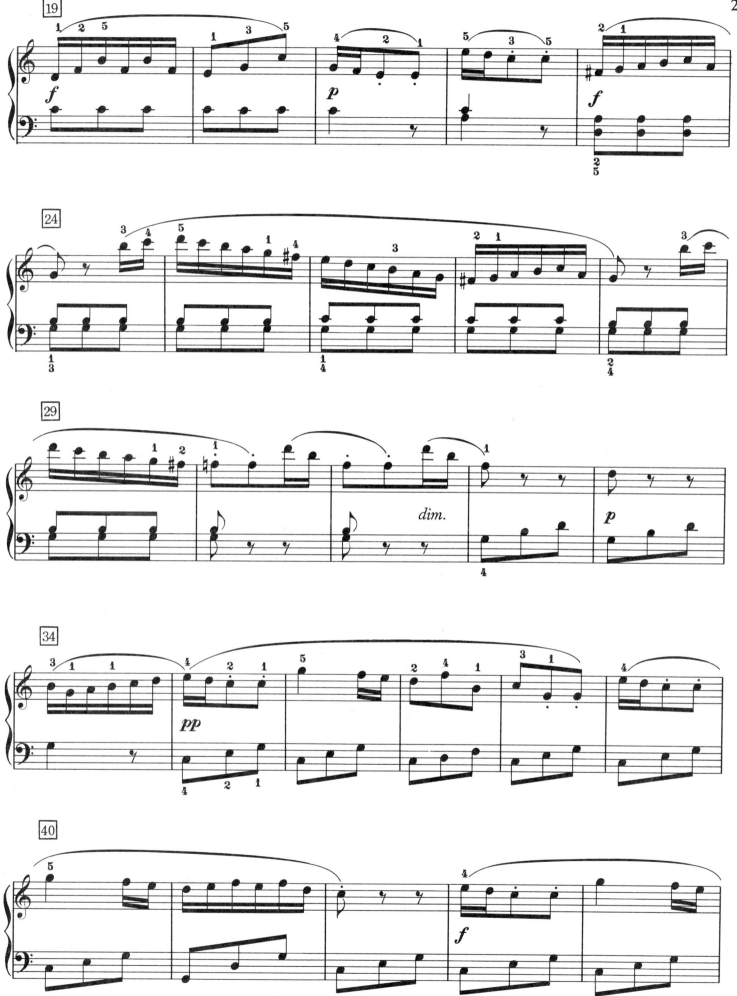

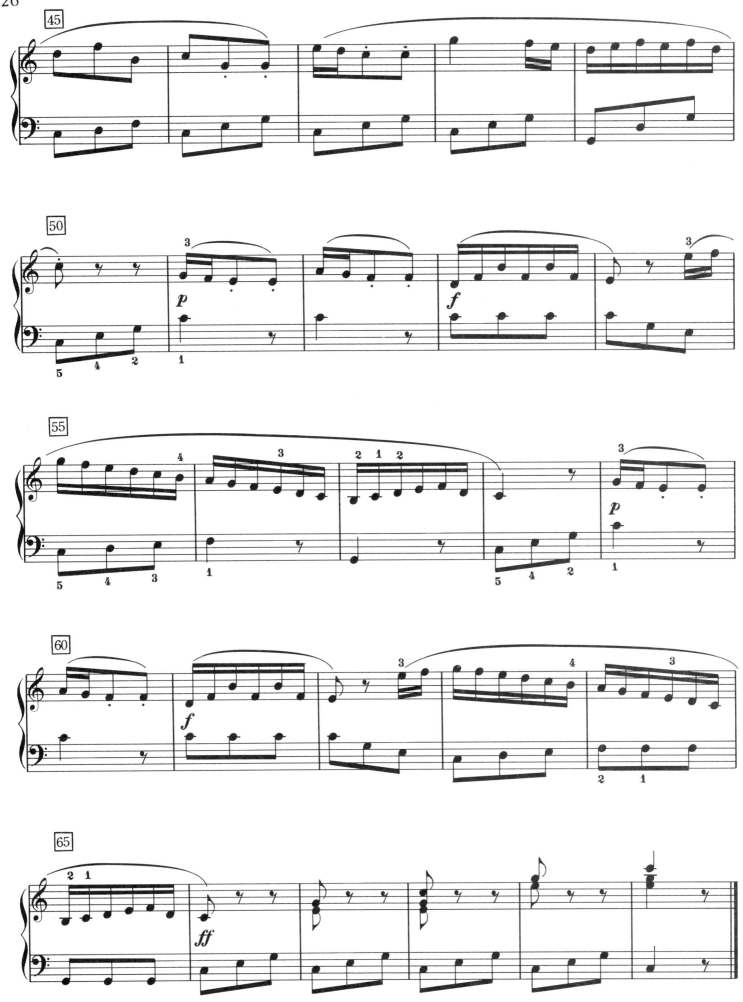

Sonatina in D Major

Ignaz Joseph Pleyel
(1757-1831)

Ignaz Joseph Pleyel was an eminent pianist and composer of his day. He studied first with Wanhal, then with Haydn. He manufactured the famous Pleyel piano, which Chopin is said to have preferred above all other makes.

Rondo
Allegro

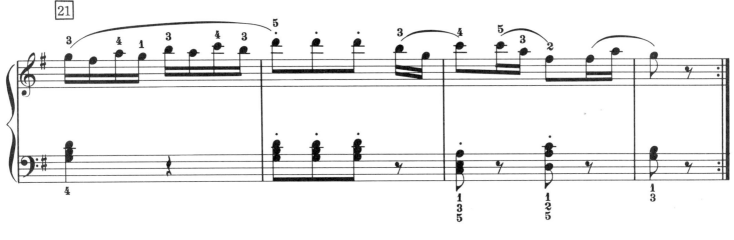

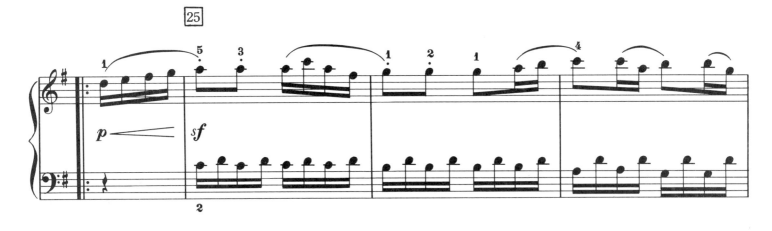

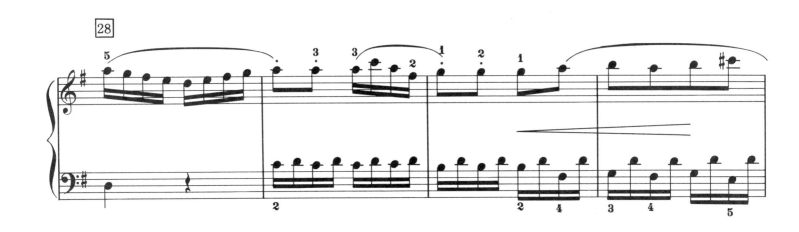